CREATING FANTASY ART

How To Draw EPIC Fantasy Art

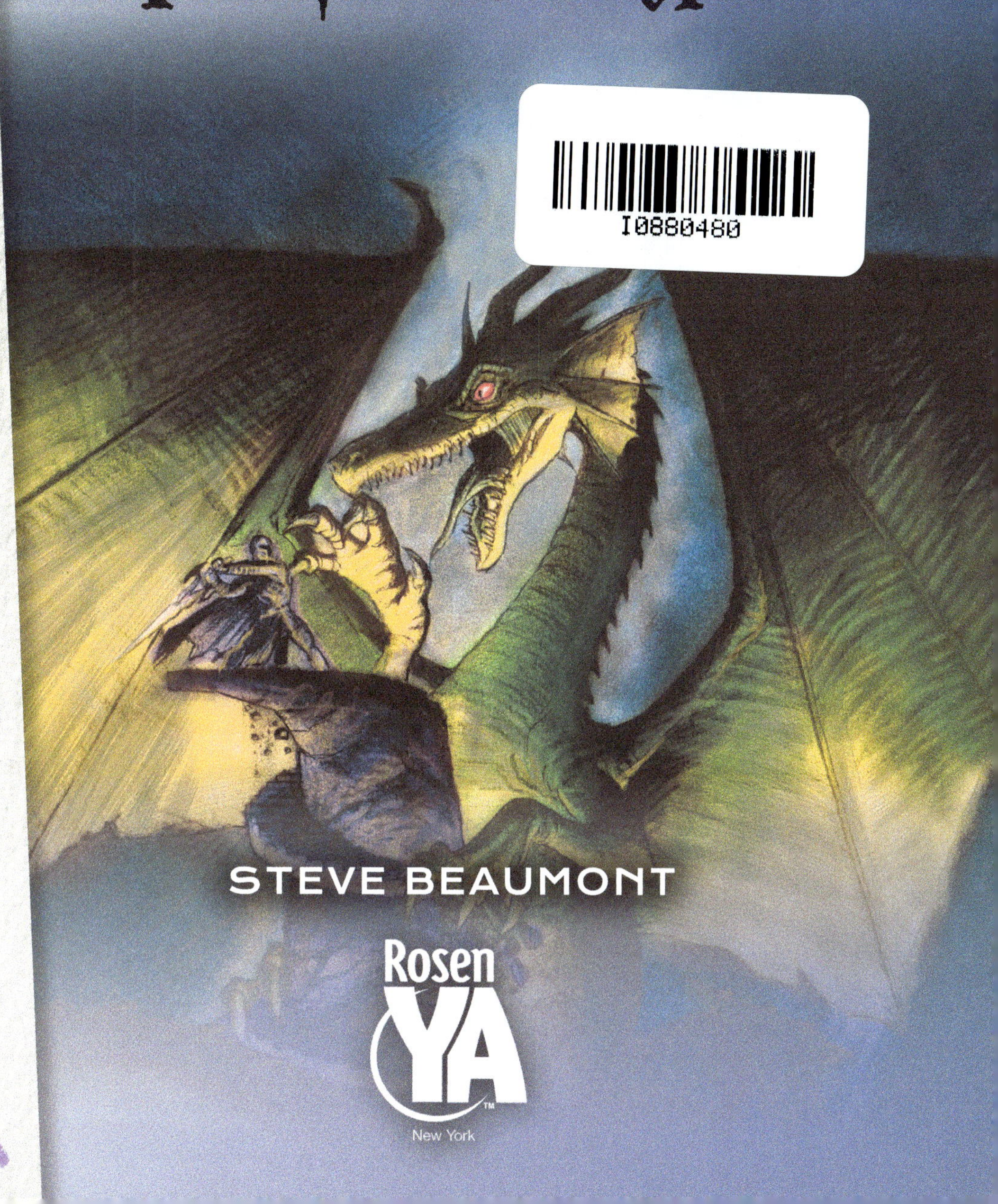

STEVE BEAUMONT

Rosen YA
New York

Published in 2018 by
The Rosen Publishing Group, Inc.
29 East 21st Street
New York, NY 10010

Library of Congress Cataloging-in-Publication Data

Names: Beaumont, Steve, author.
Title: How to draw epic fantasy art / Steve Beaumont.
Description: New York : Rosen Publishing, 2018. | Series: Creating fantasy art | Includes bibliographical references and index. | Audience: Grades 7–12.
Identifiers: LCCN 2017002345| ISBN 9781499466706 (library-bound) | ISBN 9781499466737 (pbk.) | ISBN 9781499466683 (6-pack)
Subjects: LCSH: Fantasy in art—Juvenile literature. | Drawing—Technique—Juvenile literature.
Classification: LCC NC825.F25 B42 2017 | DDC 741.2—dc23
LC record available at https://lccn.loc.gov/2017002345

Manufactured in the United States of America

All illustrations are original. Credits for additional images: Shutterstock: 19, 20, 28

CONTENTS

Introduction

As a child, I liked nothing better than losing myself in a sci-fi or horror movie or a pile of superhero comics. My favorite films were the ones that featured creatures created by Ray Harryhausen and included *Jason and the Argonauts*, *One Million Years BC* and *The Golden Voyage of Sinbad*, in which, for me, the animated characters rather than the actors played the starring roles.

These stop-motion model animation (dynamation as it became known) movies had a huge impact on me, as did the work of Jack Kirby, the legendary comic book artist, and Frank Frazetta, whose work I still regard today as the best in fantasy art. Indeed, I believe that had I not been impressed by Jack Kirby's art work and wanted to copy it, I may never have picked up a pencil and started to draw. Unfortunately my passion for fantasy art, sci-fi and comics was not shared by the teachers at my school, who considered it to be a futile pursuit.

It was my dream to go to art college and learn to draw to a professional standard, but a series of events shattered those dreams and I never did get that opportunity. However, my love of fantasy art did not die and I continued to watch fantasy movies and read superhero comics, which inspired me to create my own fantasy art. I believe art college is a good place to develop your skills as an illustrator and education is paramount, but I do not think that it is the only path to success in illustration. My own experience

Skeleton soldier from the 1963 fantasy feature film *Jason and the Argonauts*, created by Ray Harryhausen.

has shown me that determination, a love of drawing and continuous practice will get you there in the end. Indeed, the purpose of this book is to encourage others to develop their fantasy art drawing skills, whether they have been lucky enough to have had an education in art or not.

This book is an entry-level guide to fantasy art. For the most part all you will need is a decent set of pencils, an eraser and some good-quality paper, as most of the exercises in this volume were produced with exactly those materials. All the exercises can be executed with varying levels of success depending on how much work you are prepared to put in. It all comes down to practice and attention to detail, which in turn comes from being observant and willing to learn. I wasn't born being able to draw the way I can now (as you can see from my childhood drawing); my skills developed over time and required practice, imagination and a lot of resolve. I am now a freelance artist producing illustrations, concept art and storyboards for the film, television and video game industries, and I have illustrated a number of graphic novels. The tutorials in this book are based on fantasy art classes that I teach at Swarthmore Learning Center, Leeds (UK).

Although the purpose of this book is for you to have fun discovering the possibilities of fantasy art, it may also awaken talents that could lead to something more. Whatever the future holds, I hope that the book will inspire you to pick up a pencil and create some wild imaginings too.

Drawn by Steve Beaumont, aged 6.

Figure Drawing

The job of a fantasy artist is to make the unreal seem real and the unbelievable, believable. Almost all fantasy art contains human or human-like figures, whether these are 'normal' or distorted beings or some kind of creature that walks on two legs. They can all be drawn with more conviction if the artist is familiar with basic anatomy.

BASIC ANATOMY

A study of the human skeleton is essential, but it is not necessary to know the names of every single bone. Nor do you have to draw a full skeleton every time you sketch a figure; by studying the structure you can simplify it and break it down into some basic shapes. The key is to get the proportions correct.

The image on the left (Figure 1) shows a human skeleton, and the image on the right (Figure 2) shows how this can be broken down into a more manageable frame, which can then be used as the basis of a figure. At this stage, the limbs can be represented by simple stick lines and the rib cage and hips as basic oval shapes.

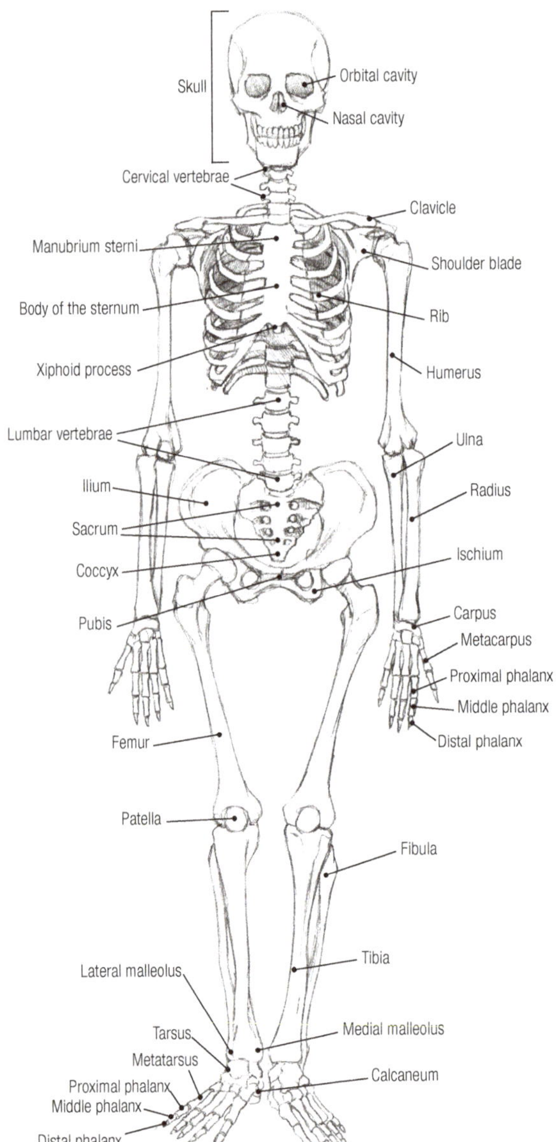

Figure 1

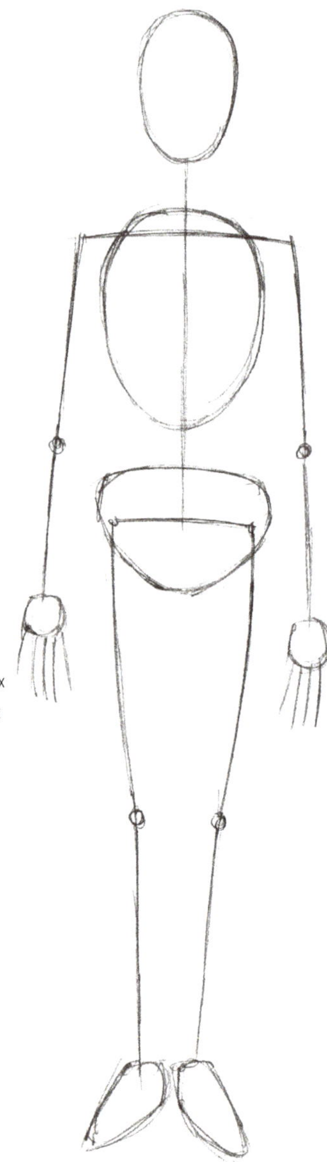

Figure 2

FIGURES IN ACTION

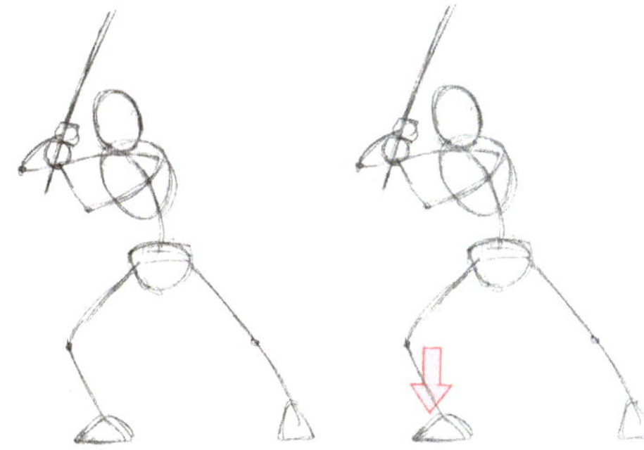

Once you are familiar with the skeleton, try drawing some rough sketches of stick figures in action. If you are drawing someone throwing a punch or swinging a sword, try to imagine the action and the direction of movement, and where the body weight is distributed. For instance, if the figure is throwing a punch it is more than likely that all the body weight will be supported by the leg that is farthest forward rather than by the rear leg.

You also need to consider the flow of movement and action. This flow can be simplified by a single stroke of a pen. This is evident when you look at the images of the upright figure with the staff in its left hand (below); one is annotated with arrows that indicate the direction of the twists and bends of the body, while in the alternative image the line of the pose has been simplified to a brush stroke.

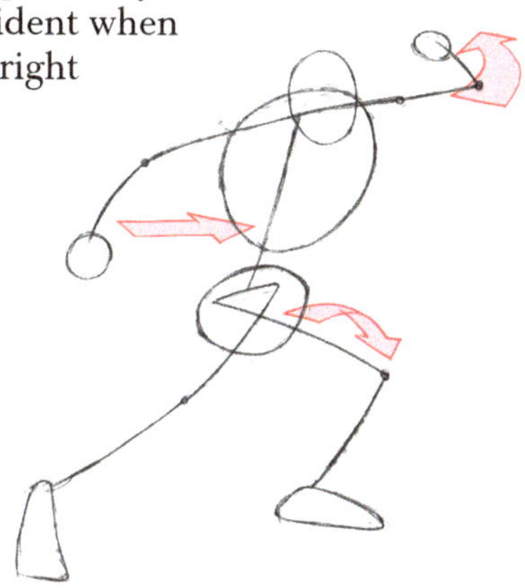

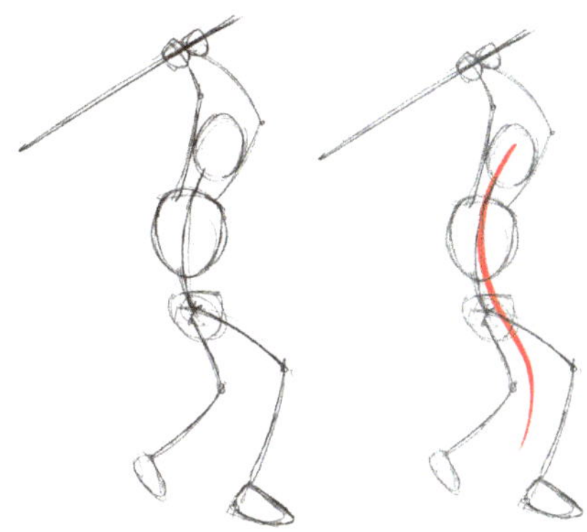

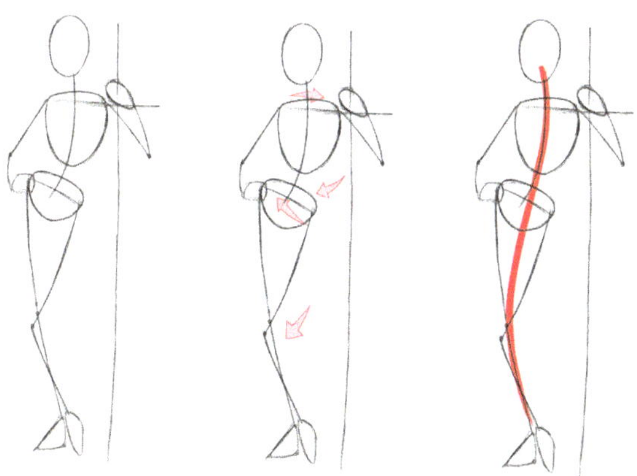

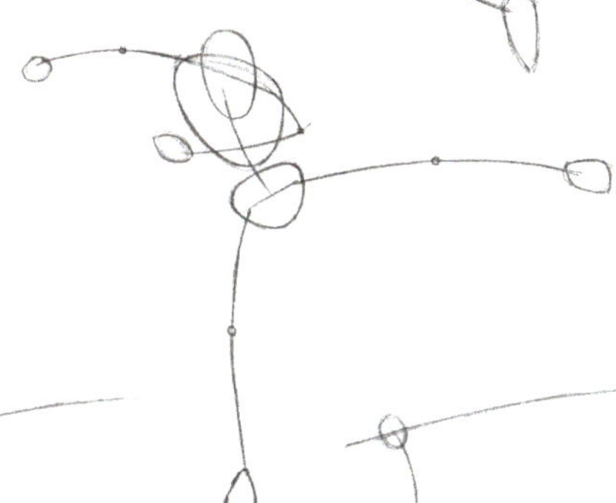

Tribal Warrior

This is an exercise in character development, inking and coloring. Learning to develop a figure from nothing other than ideas in your head is an important process in fantasy art. When I have been commissioned to create a character, whether for a video game or as concept art for a film, I go through a process of making a collection of rough sketches. Each of these explores a direction of thought and how the character could look, and the final design will sometimes be a combination of different parts of each concept sketch. This is probably the most fun part of creating fantasy art as you don't always know where the chain of thought will take you.

STEP 1

Here we have a collection of sketches that show the various stages of development for a character. I began by scribbling out a rough skeleton to determine the pose of the figure. I decided that he will be carrying a weapon which I roughly indicated with a stick.

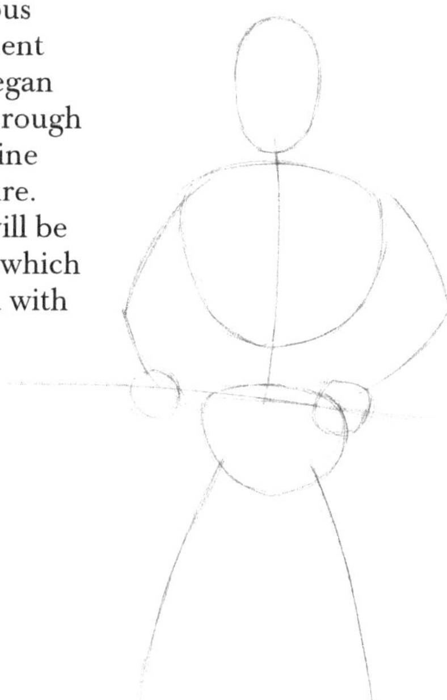

STEP 2

The next stage is to decide on the build of the character, exploring whether the body will be muscular or slightly built.

STEP 3

Having chosen the body shape, it is time to add detail to the figure and to settle on the type of weapon. For this exercise I have chosen an axe for the warrior to wield, but you can opt for whichever weapon you like (Figure 1 shows an alternative).

Figure 1

STEP 4

It is now time to explore different ideas that may or may not enhance the look of the warrior. Here I have begun by applying a tribal tattoo on his arm and the side of his face and head.

STEP 5

I decided to give my character a ponytail as an addition to his bald head, which meant that all of the tattoo would still be visible. I felt that the design of the axe was a bit weak, so I developed this further to create a more interesting weapon.

ADDING ARMOR

Consider trying out a helmet and other types of body armor. This particular concept sketch illustrates that I have applied too much armor, resulting in elements that conflict with each other. This is not a good example of balanced design. You need to look at the armor you have added and check that elements work cohesively.

Figure 2

Play around with the different elements until you get it right. In this image I have erased the shoulder armor and added a cloak pin. This simplifies the design – it is less cluttered and there are no conflicting components. Remember, sometimes less is more!

Figure 3

STEP 6

Having been through the development process you should have a figure that you are happy with, and can now go ahead and apply ink. I have chosen to ink the original tribal warrior, without the armor and with the tattoo, as I felt it was the better character design of the two. The starkness of his mostly bald head allows you to focus on his fierce stare and facial scar. Also, because he has no armor, the scars on his body are visible, making him look more brutal. You may want to start inking the most interesting part of the drawing first, which for me is the head. I used a superfine pen for the facial details, especially the eyes.

STEP 7

A superfine pen can also be used for the hatching, as shown. I applied more pressure to the nib at the beginning of the stroke to create a heavier line, and gradually released the pressure towards the end to create a lighter line. This is best executed in a quick stroke, so do not think too much about how much pressure to apply at the beginning and the end. It is best to practice a few times on a scrap sheet of paper first.

STEP 8

Once you have completed the head, move on to other areas. I continued with the superfine pen for the hair and scars (Figure 4) and then finished off the solid black areas using a brush pen. Using an actual brush and Indian ink would do the job just as well. Notice that I have applied a thicker weight of line on the underside of muscles such as the chest (pectorals) and biceps and embellished them with hatching to create the appearance of roundness of shape.

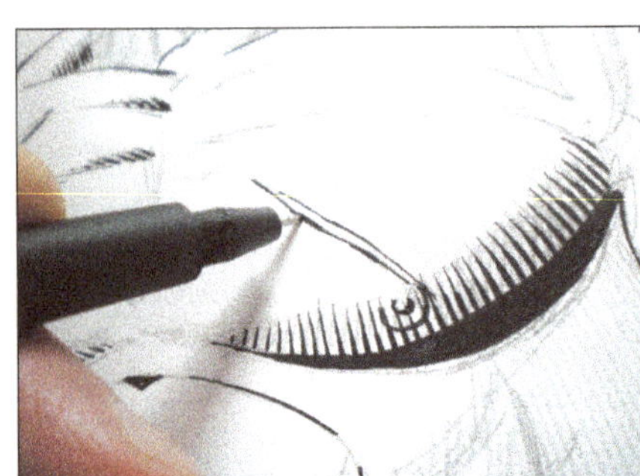

Figure 4

STEP 9

You may have to pause and consider different options during the inking process. In this case, I was not certain whether to ink the tattoos in solid black or to sketch them in thin line to be filled in with a colored pen later, or even to leave the arm blank and draw the tattoo with a coloring pen. Leaving the tattoo in outline (as shown here) would make it easier to color by keeping the color within a confined space. Applying the tattoo with a colored pen, however, would give an appealing finish. In the end I chose to ink in the tattoo using solid black, which looks powerful and also works well once the rest of the drawing has been colored (Figure 5, below).

Figure 5

STEP 10

You can now move on to coloring the picture. To color this drawing I primarily used Copic markers. I began by laying down the base layers of skin tone, hair, clothing and the weapon. For the skin, I used Copic E53 Raw Silk and a Blush Letraset Pro marker (Figure 6). For the hair, leather straps and belt I used Copic E39 Leather. For the protective leather straps hanging from the belt I used Copic E35 Chamois (Figure 7), and for the loincloth I used Copic E09 Burnt Sienna (Figure 8).

Figure 6

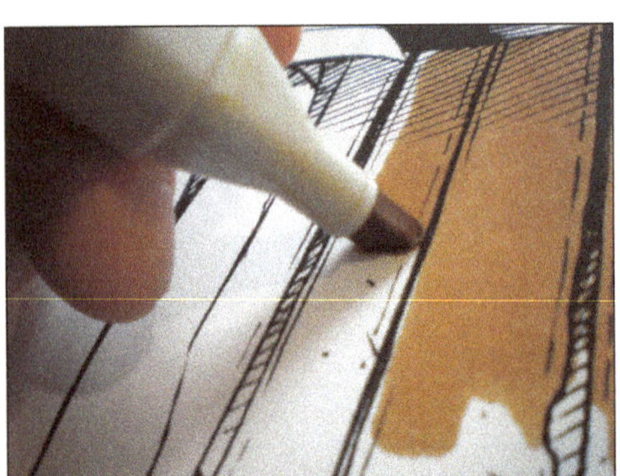

Figure 7

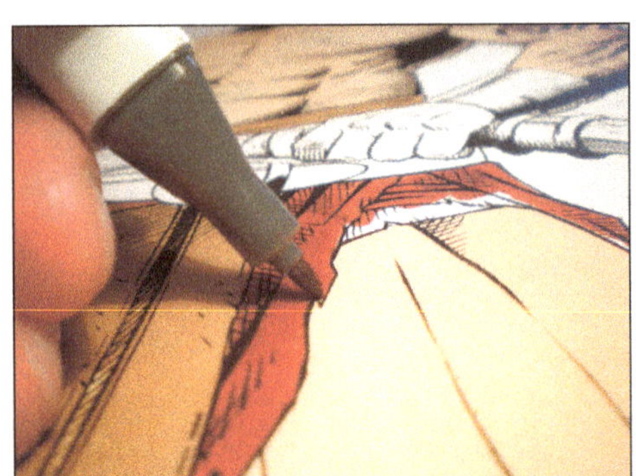

Figure 8

STEP II

The base layer of color should then be built upon using layers of darker tones. Lighter, subtle tones can be achieved by using the same color marker over the base layer once it has dried. Start by finishing the skin layers. Here I used Copic E53 Raw Silk, E11 Barely Beige and E31 Brick Beige (Figure 9 and Figure 10).

Figure 9

Figure 10

STEP 12

Having worked on the skin tones, turn your attention to the weapon, clothing and armor. I built the warmer tones of the axe head using Copic Y15 (Cadmium Yellow) and Y21 (Buttercup Yellow). The darker tones of the loincloth (Figure 11), leather (Figure 12) and hair (Figure 13) were created by adding a layer of E27 (Africano) followed by a layer of Copic W5 (Warm Grey). I did not want the leather to have a totally smooth appearance, so I purposely created an uneven layer by applying more of the Warm Grey in some areas than in others to create a worn effect. Using a marker with a nib that is drying up is good for this effect.

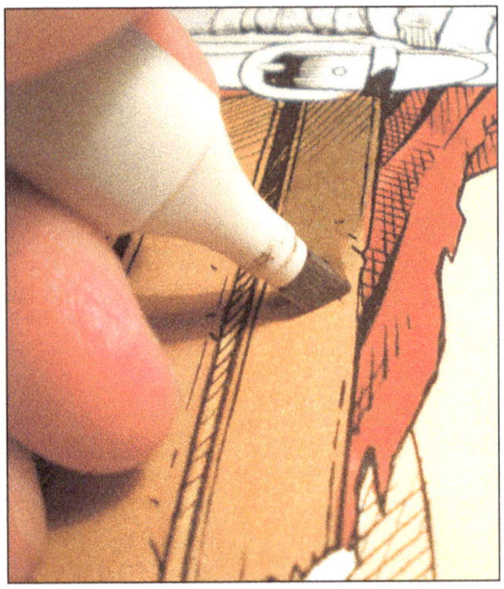

Figure 11

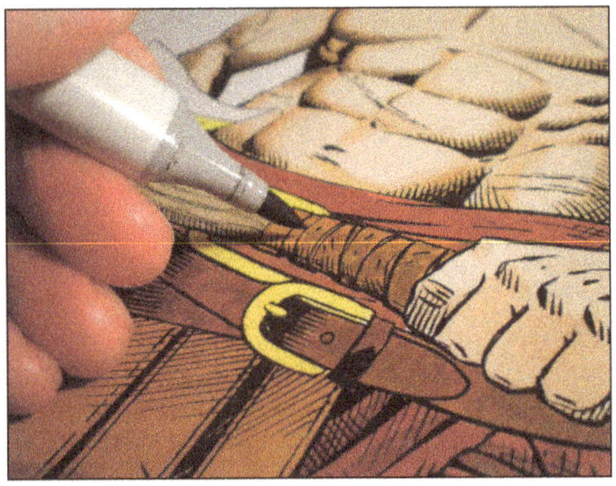

Figure 12

Figure 13

STEP 13

Finally, add the finishing touches to blend the colors. I applied a Copic W2 (Warm Grey 2) and W3 (Warm Grey 3) to the parts of the skin I wanted to appear darker, in particular the left side (as we are looking at him) of the figure, the head, shoulder, shadowed areas of the hands and the outer line of the leg – basically anywhere where there was shadow that I felt needed some extra tone to blend lighter and darker areas. I used some thinned white gouache to make the scar tissue more prominent. I used a Copic W3 to add extra tone to the axe head.

PIRATE

During my childhood I saw many seafaring adventure movies. Some were sci-fi movies, such as *Twenty Thousand Leagues under the Sea* and *It Came From Beneath the Sea,* and some were 'high adventure' movies, such as *Treasure Island* and *Moby Dick.* The visual imagery of these and more modern feature films, such as Walt Disney's *Pirates of the Caribbean,* has had a strong impact on me and informs much of my artwork. Pirates, giant sea monsters and other supernatural creatures all make for great fantasy art and this exercise combines elements of all three.

Figure 1

Before embarking on a piece of art it is good practice to produce some quick, rough sketches to determine the layout of your proposed work. In the professional world of illustration these rough sketches are known as thumbnails. They help an artist explore a number of concepts in a short space of time, using a minimal amount of expensive materials. I began this exercise by sketching a few thumbnail layouts to explore various compositions, before settling for the one that worked best (Figure 1).

Figure 4

Having decided upon the composition of the picture as a whole, you need to think about what the main character will look like. The kind of pirate I had in mind was a person with dreadlocks. I sourced a few photo references (Figure 2 and Figure 3) and produced some quick character sketches (Figure 4 and Figure 5) to determine the look of my figure.

Figure 2

Figure 3

Figure 5

STEP 1

Generally, when a professional artist begins to work up a piece of art from a thumbnail, he or she will either enlarge the thumbnail using a photocopier or by scanning it, opening it on a computer and increasing its size there. However, if you do not have access to these facilities then it is best to redraw the image from scratch at the correct size. Drawing a faint centerline on both the thumbnail image and the larger piece of paper will help you balance your layout.
Start by loosely sketching the body, the stance of the pirate and the flow of the tentacles around him. Notice how the two largest tentacles are framing the character; this is a method used by many artists to draw attention to the main point of interest. Also roughly sketch out a pile of skulls at the pirate's feet.

STEP 2

The next step is to sketch out the clothing. It may be a good idea to search the Internet to see what reference material you can find, or maybe watch a few pirate movies. You can also find lots of scenes from movies on the Internet.

STEP 3

Now you can start to develop the details of the clothing and weapons and begin to draw the face.

ADDING DETAIL TO THE TENTACLES AND SKULLS

Tentacles

To draw convincing tentacles it will be helpful to study some reference material, such as this picture of an octopus (Figure 6). Notice that the tentacles have two rows of suction cups and that they are not all perfectly aligned. The drawing will look more interesting if the suction cups are a bit irregular and point off in different directions, but make sure that they fit with the curves and twists of the tentacle (Figure 7).

Figure 6

Figure 7

Skulls

Study the photo of the skull (Figure 8) and you will notice there are curves and recesses around the eye sockets and also around the cheekbones. These shapes will differ from skull to skull so you do not have to be too accurate. Most adults have roughly 14–15 teeth on each row, but this varies and, when drawing a skull from the front, remember that the back teeth are not visible. When drawing an ancient-looking skull, removing some of the teeth gives the skull a more weathered look.

Drawing skulls is similar to drawing a face, but a bit easier, and it is best to start by practicing a few on a separate piece of paper. First, draw a circle, then divide it into quarters and draw a square roughly below the center line (Figure 9). Now add the eye sockets and a hole for the nose, and indicate the position of the mouth (Figure 10). The eyes are basically irregular-shaped circles. Try not to make them too perfectly round – notice there are flat parts too. The nose is like a triangle with rounded edges. Add the teeth (Figure 11), then shade in the eye sockets and nose (Figure 12).

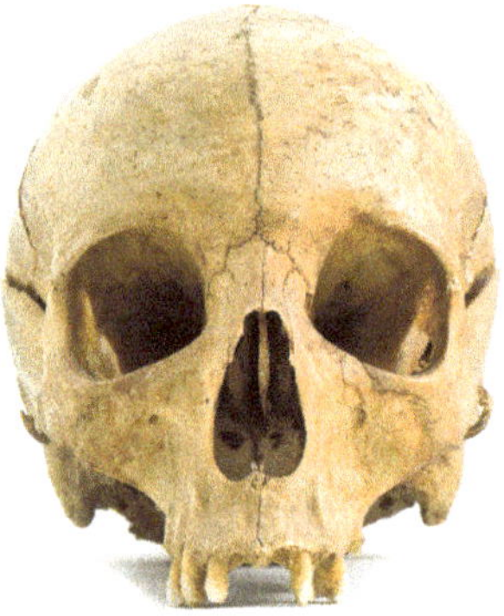

Figure 8

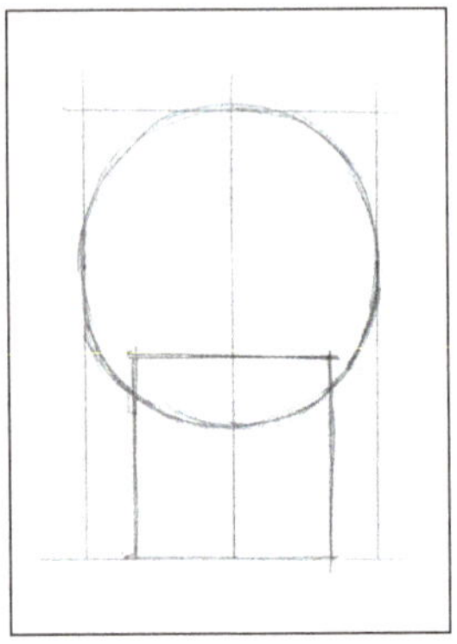

Figure 9

Figure 10

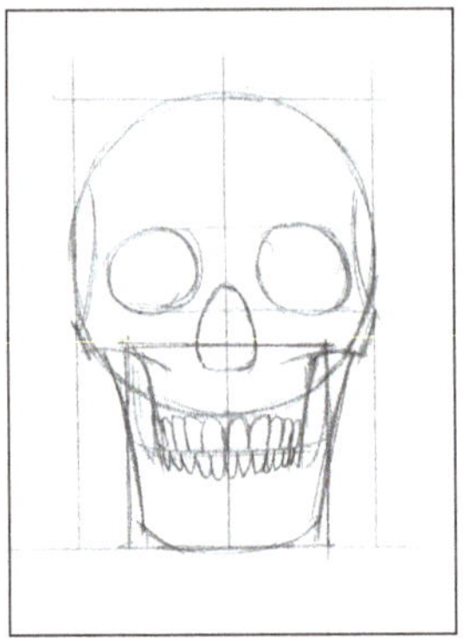

Figure 11

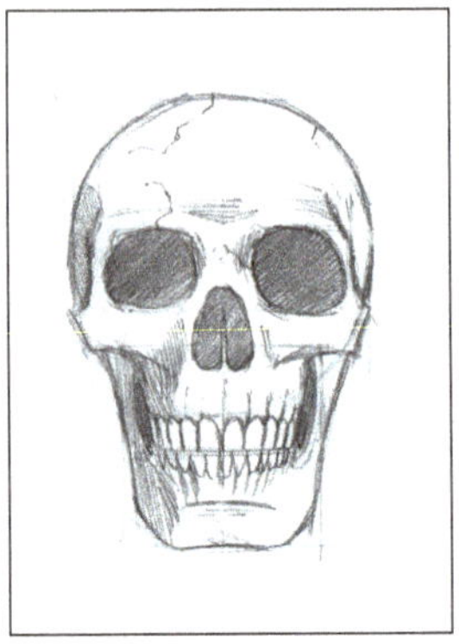

Figure 12

STEP 4
Once you are happy you can draw a skull, add the details to the pile of them at the pirate's feet. Aim to draw the skulls in an irregular arrangement, overlapping and placed at different angles.

STEP 5

Add the final details to the tentacles, paying attention to the suction cups and making sure that they do not look too aligned and symmetrical – they should look natural. The details on the skulls should also vary slightly so that they do not all look the same. One of the keys to creating convincing artwork is to make it appear as natural as possible. The more mechanical and precise it seems, the less realistic it looks (unless you happen to be drawing machinery, in which case, be precise).

STEP 6

You can now begin the shading. I started by shading the main areas in shadow, such as the folds of the clothing and the underside of the tentacles, as well as the hair, which is not in shadow but which I wanted to be a mass of black.

STEP 7

Blend the pencil work to create a smoother finish, and begin to add the mid-range tones to the clothing and tentacles using a blending stump or tissue paper (Figure 13).

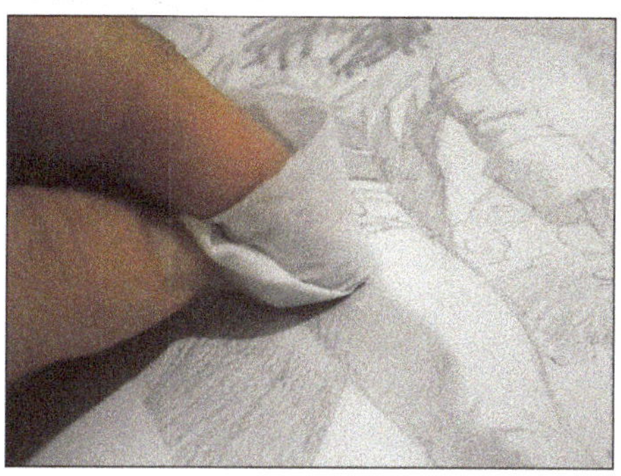

Figure 13

STEP 8

For the background I wanted to create ambiguous cloudy shapes that could either be sky or steam, like clouds of mist rising from the water and around the tentacles. Use an HB pencil to create some cloud-like shapes and blend them together with your finger, using circular motions. Add some extra layers of pencil in places and blend these to create the effect of moving clouds of mist. I found using a piece of tissue worked better than a blending stump. Add some tonal shading to the skulls and blend it to create an overall tone, so you can create highlights with an eraser later on.

STEP 9

Create the skin detail on the tentacles by blending layers of pencil, then apply fine line work over the top, drawing tightly grouped squiggles and swirls (Figures 14 and 15).

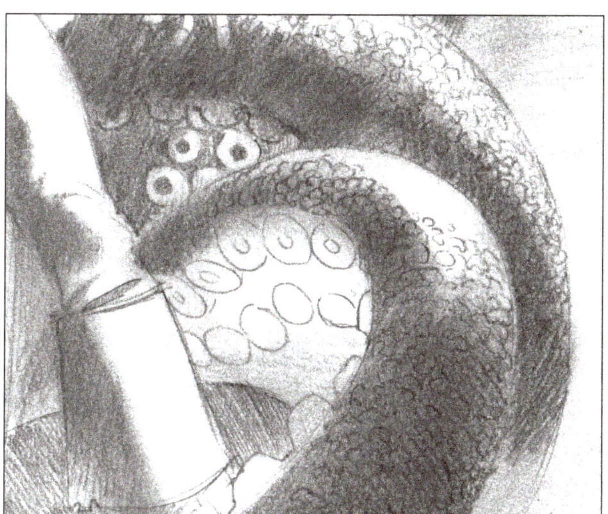

Figure 14

Figure 15

STEP 10

Having added detail to the outer skin of the tentacles, the underside now needs to be developed. This can be done by drawing irregular lines across the width between and around the suction cups, using the flat edge of a pencil (Figure 16). Sourcing some photos of water ripples (Figures 17 and 18) will enable you to create the water effect shown in the drawing opposite.

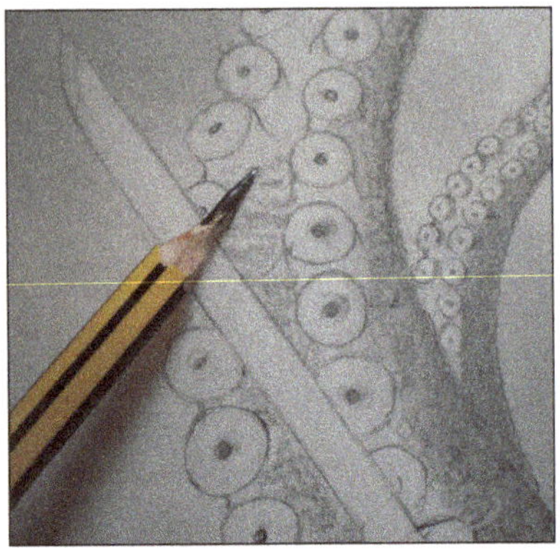

Figure 16

Figure 17

Figure 18

Here you can see that the drawing is almost finished. All it needs now are highlights and some swirling mist.

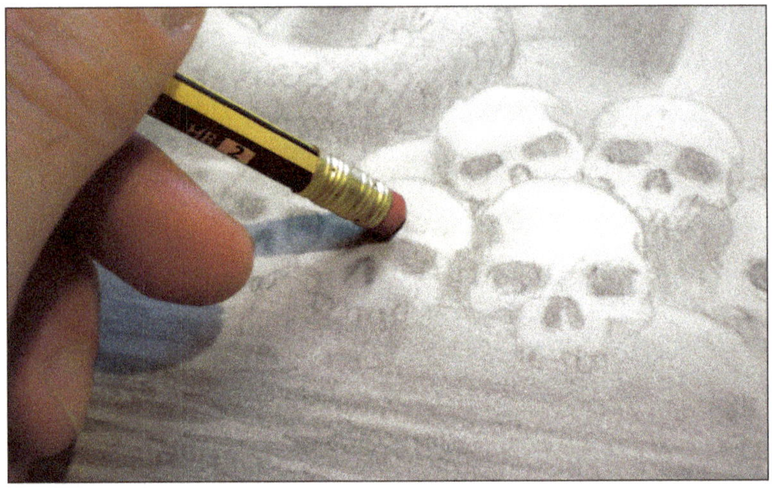

STEP 11
Before creating the swirling mist you should apply highlights to all areas that are looking a bit flat and need emphasizing. Use an eraser to add them to the right-hand side of each skull, and add some mottled highlights to the curves of the tentacles and some of the suction cups.

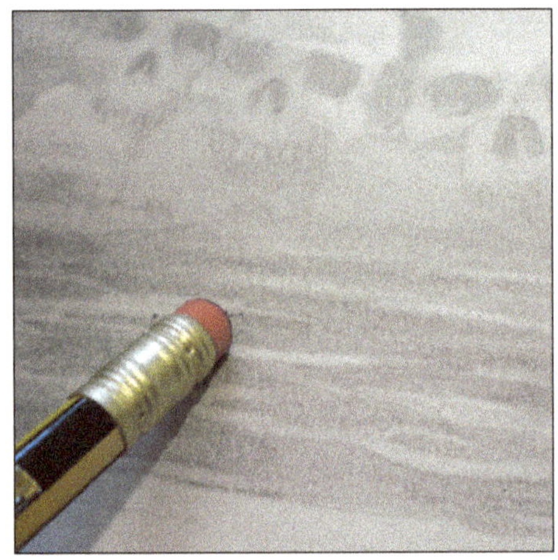

Figure 19

STEP 12
Some additional darker pencil work can be used to strengthen the ripples before highlights are added with an eraser (Figure 19).

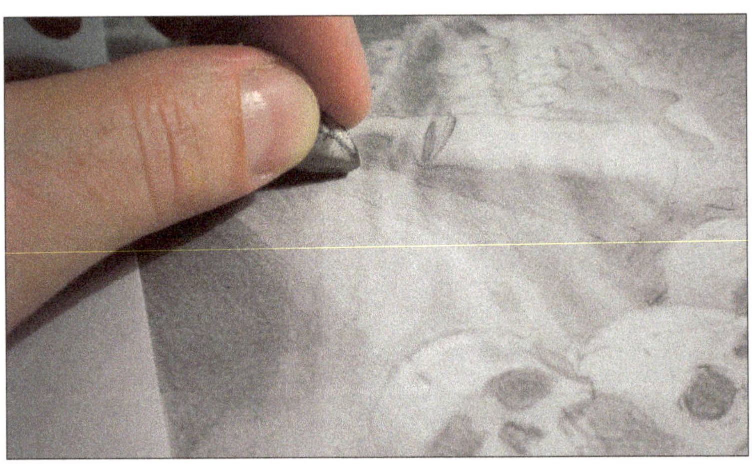

STEP 13
Leave the mist until last, so that it is applied over the highlights, to create a more believable effect. I achieved this by dragging a stump of a well-worn eraser over the skulls, around the tentacles and behind and in front of the legs. Finally, if there are any parts of the drawing that need defining, apply a crisp pencil line with an HB pencil. You can see the completed drawing on the facing page.

Dragon's Lair

Featuring in the mythology of many countries – including Japan, China, England, Wales, Scotland, France and South America – dragons are one of the most recognized and frequently depicted creatures in fantasy art. Although they are sometimes portrayed as the guardians of fabulous treasure and secret gateways to hidden lands, these memorable beasts are more often shown wreaking havoc on villages and castles or locked in fierce combat with a heroic warrior. For this drawing I have chosen the latter scenario.

This exercise will draw upon the disciplines of figure drawing, composition and lighting and requires a pencil and a piece of paper. I used a Staedtler HB pencil on Winsor & Newton 300gsm cartridge paper.

Before jumping straight into the action I thought it would be helpful, for those of you who have not drawn a dragon before, to look at how relatively easy it is. Also, it will be a good warm-up exercise to prepare you for the main drawing.
I usually start any drawing by producing rough, loose sketches, keeping the line work light so that I can continue to draw over the top of it (Figure 1). I find reducing a subject to simplified shapes can be helpful while you are becoming acquainted with a new form, so I have shown here how the form can be broken down using some red shapes. I have not gone for the usual circles, blocks and cylinders – instead I have roughly drawn an oval for the body and created some pleasing curves for the tail and neck (Figure 2). When sketching the shapes, keep them loose and rough. Try not to become too involved with drawing the shapes – remember you are drawing a dragon, and that is your focus (Figure 3). Try to let the lines flow. Once you have created a natural-looking pose that you are happy with, you can start to develop the sketch further by adding more detail (Figures 4 and 5).

Figure 1

Figure 2

Figure 3

Figure 4

Figure 5

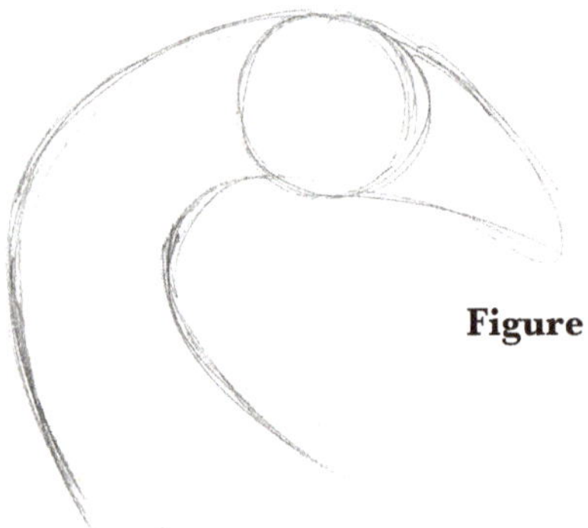
Figure 6

This section examines how to develop the head. This is easier than you may think; it's just a tapered shape that comprises a semi-triangular tip and a sphere, all put together in a pleasingly fluid curved form (Figure 6). You can then add the basic structures of the eye, jaw line, mouth, nose and any spikes or horns (Figures 7 and 8). As I child I was a dinosaur-fanatic and they have continued to fascinate me as an adult. Structurally similar to most representations of dragons, dinosaurs are the obvious reference for an exercise such as this one and can greatly assist the imaginative process. For the head, I looked at some of the big flesh-eating dinosaurs that feature in Steven Spielberg's *Jurassic Park* movies. Studying some dinosaur skulls was also helpful when it came to deciding on the shape of the eyes and jaw. My preference when drawing a dragon's jaw is to have the teeth visible even when the mouth is closed, a feature that can be seen in alligators and crocodiles (Figure 9). Scales and other textural details add both interest and depth to the image (Figure 10).

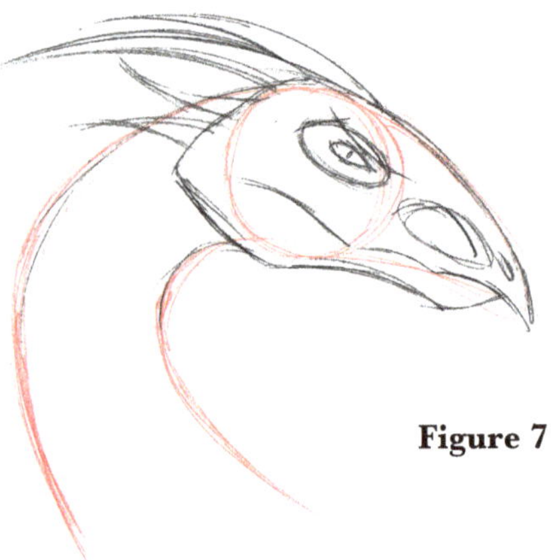
Figure 7

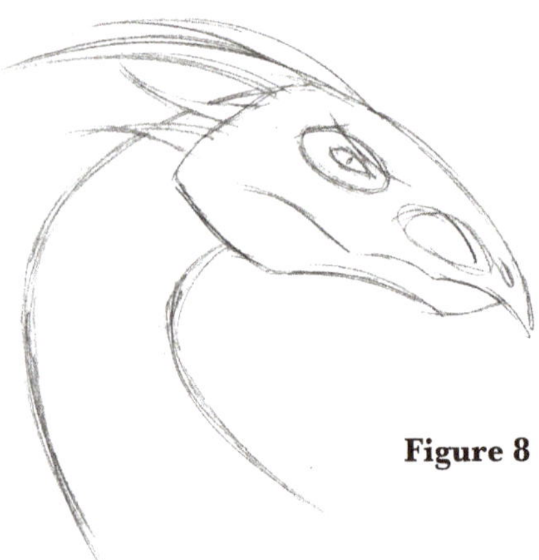
Figure 8

Figure 9

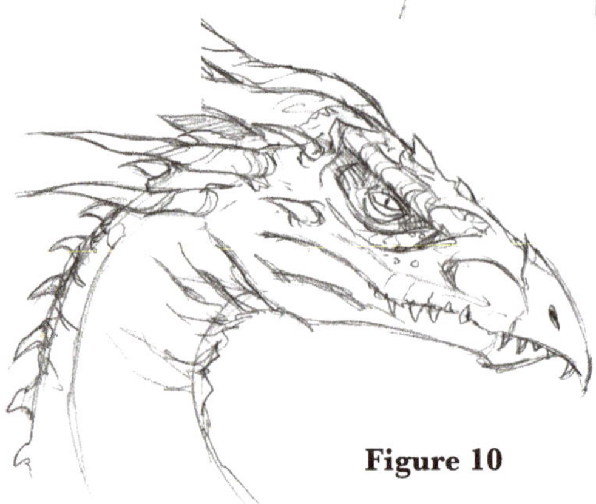
Figure 10

Figure 11

Figure 12

Figures 11–14 are the rough thumbnails and concepts explored in the thought process that helped me arrive at the final image. In most of the roughs (not all of them are featured here) the wings were used to draw the viewer in to the center of the image, where the action is taking place. The ever-reliable, tried-and-tested framing devices of a large sphere and a pillar of smoke were used to isolate the shape of the dragon and draw attention to the action. Although I liked the close-up, intense image in Figure 11, its composition didn't leave space for much scenery. Since this book focuses not only on the figures but also the environments that complete the picture and provide mood and atmosphere, I felt that a wider shot was necessary which incorporated both a full-figure dragon and its setting.

Figure 13

Figure 14

STEP 1

Start by plotting out the content of the layout. For the purposes of clarity I have adjusted the strength of the line work so that it prints clearly, but I recommend you keep the rough plotting light so that it can easily be corrected with an eraser and you can work over the top of it successfully. You will notice that all the elements are composed around a central vertical line. The dragon's head is at a very slight angle so the inside of its mouth will be visible. If it helps, think of the head as a tapered rectangle shape, roughly drawing the sides as I have done, then build the features around it.

STEP 2

Add the limbs, tail and wings to the dragon. Wrapping the tail around the stone ruin enables the dragon to further dominate the scene, and the wings provide a framing device. Pay attention to the form of the feet and hands, as these can be difficult to perfect. If necessary, practice sketching them on a scrap of paper before adding them to the artwork.

STEP 3

Begin to add more detail to the dragon and the ruin, taking time carefully to plot the steps winding round it. Notice that I have added other points of narrative interest, such as the dragon's claw demolishing a section of the steps, to suggest that this is a final battle, a point of no return for the warrior. You can also start to plot the foreground using a low point of perspective. The skulls in the foreground do not follow the perspective lines, as the ground is uneven and full of sunken areas. I chose to place skulls in the foreground to suggest that many had tried and failed to conquer the beast.

STEP 4

Take a look at the composition. Do the elements work well? What is the focus of the drawing? I decided that although the skulls were a nice feature, my eye was drawn too much to them and I wanted it to be focused on the main point of interest – the battle scene. I removed most of them, leaving one at the bottom right as a reminder of previous defeats. I decided to draw the ground as broken and floating on a bed of molten lava, to make the environment even more perilous. Notice that I have adjusted the angle of the steps at the base of the ruin. At this stage, if your drawing is looking a bit grubby, you might want to trace it on to a clean sheet of paper using a lightbox, if you have one.

STEP 5

In order to begin shading the outline, you need to identify where the light source is coming from so that you can determine which areas are highlighted and which are in shadow. In this instance, since the ground is lava – a source of intense heat – it makes sense for the lighting to come from below, creating shadows to the higher outer areas of the dragon and the scenery. Begin to shade in these areas and identify the parts that will be darkest and will anchor the image (Figure 15).

Figure 15

STEP 6

Once the darker areas have been identified, begin work on building up layers of tone over all areas of the drawing. This will act as a base layer upon which you can add layers of darker tone, more detail and textural interest. Blend together the first layers of shading to meld the pencil strokes and create a smoother overall tone. I vary my tools for blending – I may use a blending stump for smaller areas and a sheet of tissue paper wrapped round my index finger for larger areas (Figure 16).

Figure 16

STEP 7

To create the textured effect on the dragon's wings, hold the pencil at a low angle, almost flat, and run it across the paper, using any texture within the paper's surface to add to the effect. Use this same technique on the dragon's skin, applying more pressure to create darker tones.

STEP 8

Once all the textures and tones have been applied, go over the drawing with an eraser to remove any unwanted pencil marks and shading where it interferes with the clarity of the line work.

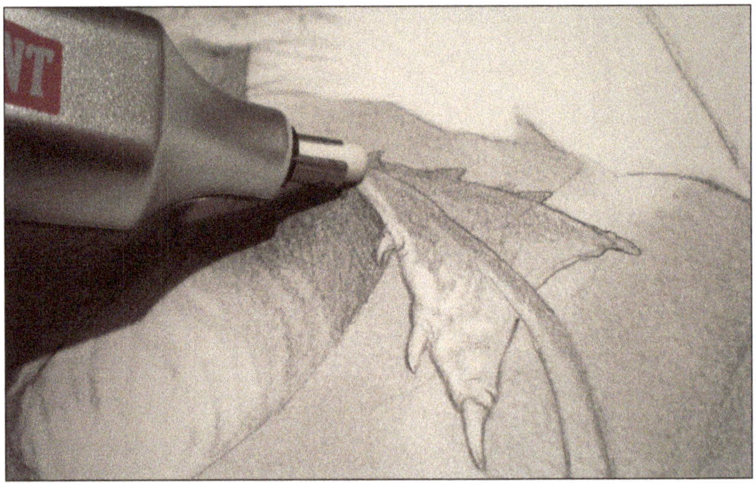

STEP 9

I also use an eraser to create highlights, which help to lift the foreground from the rest of the background tone.

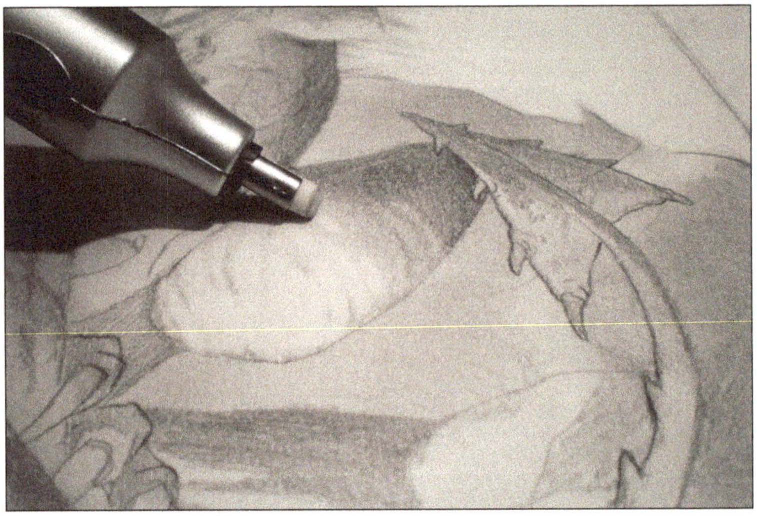

STEP 10

After creating highlights with an eraser, re-apply pencil to any of the line work that may accidentally have been erased or smudged. You need to create a defined outline that will make the dragon stand out. Use as sharp a point as you can for this. Some artists prefer to use a technical pencil for crisp line work, but a very sharp pencil will do just as well. Make sure that details such as the claws and teeth, which should look razor-sharp, are extremely crisply defined.

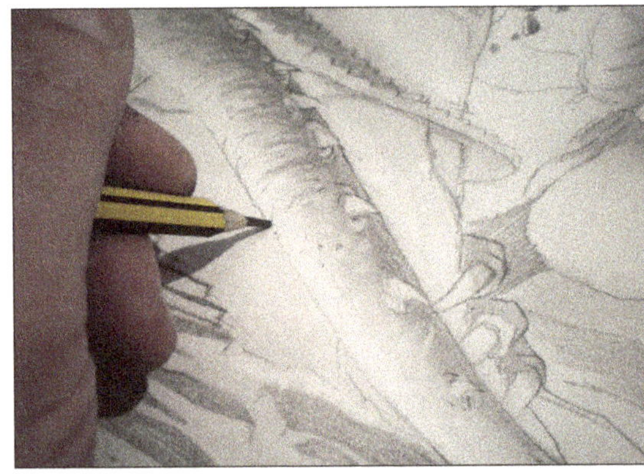

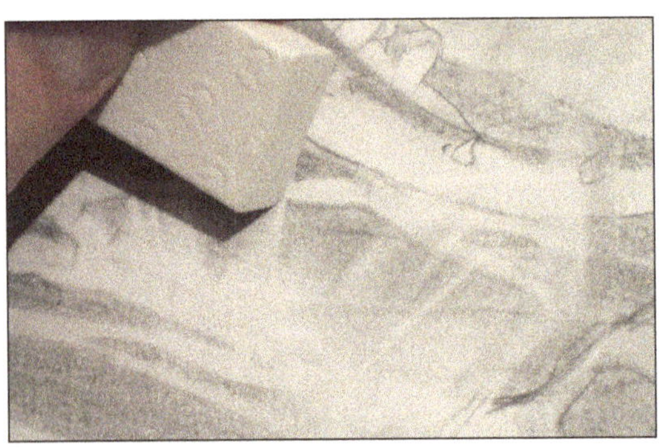

STEP 11

Use the flat edge of an eraser to add shafts of flickering light emanating from the molten lava below the dragon. The larger, flatter eraser won't totally erase the pencil work – instead it will make the shafts of light appear slightly translucent. Lastly, use a smaller eraser to create finer highlights and give the effect of flames. Sit back and assess the piece, making any last corrections or adjustments as required.

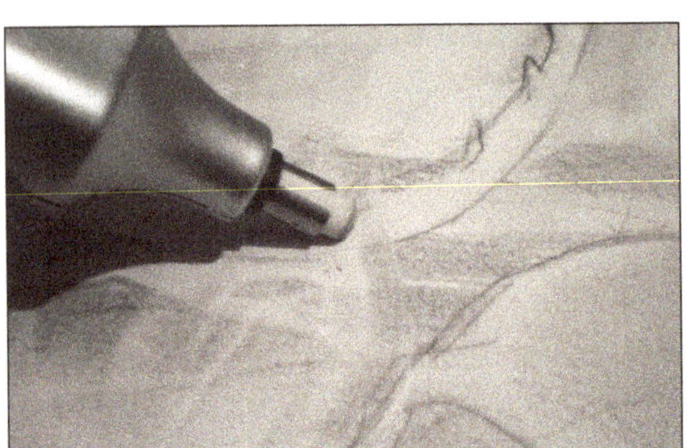

SKETCHBOOK

I often stress the importance of keeping sketchbooks to my students. They can be used for any kind of drawing – from observational sketches or the exploration of ideas to testing out new materials (pens, pencils, paints, etc.) or just doodling for the fun of it. All these activities help to develop drawing skills and, as with most things, the more you practice, the better you become. Professional artists fill dozens of sketchbooks. The rough workings of some, including Frank Frazetta, Jeffrey Jones and Claire Wendling, have been turned into high-end art books that showcase their creative processes. The seeds of some of your best ideas may be doodled in a sketchbook. Ideas flow uninhibited when you are not feeling too precious about your drawing and you may often experience a breakthrough in this way.

GLOSSARY

anatomy The body structure of humans and animals.

cohesive Two or more things that work well together.

composition The way that different elements are set together to create an overall effect.

distorted Pulled and twisted out of shape.

gouache Paint with a glue-like texture.

lightbox A flat box with a translucent top and light inside, used by artists to help when tracing pictures.

mythology A collection of stories that come from a particular culture or tradition.

observation Closely watching something or someone, noticing significant details.

sci-fi Short for science fiction.

stop-motion A type of animation created using a camera that is continually stopped and started again.

supernatural Coming from something outside or above the laws of nature.

tentacles A flexible limb of some animals.

FURTHER INFORMATION

Chris Riddell's Doodle-a-Day by Chris Riddell (Macmillan Children's Books, 2015)

Draw and Write Your Own Comics by Louie Stowell (Usborne Publishing, 2014)

Drawing Fantasy Creatures by Aaron Sautter (Capstone Press, 2016)

Drawing Manga: Step-by-Step by Ben Krefta (Arcturus Publishing, 2013)

Drawing Wizards, Witches and Warlocks by Christ Hart (Sixth and Spring Books, 2009)

How to Draw Fantasy Art by Mark Bergin (PowerKids Press, 2011)

Terry Pratchett's Discworld Colouring Book by Paul Kidby (Gollancz, 2016)

INDEX